FiREfLY JULY

A Year of Very Short Poems

selected by **PAUL B. JANECZKO**

illustrated by **MELISSA SWEET**

CANDLEWICK PRESS

CONTENTS

Spring

Summer

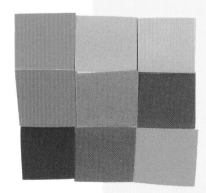

Daybreak reminds us –
the hills have arrived just in
time to celebrate.

— Cid Corman

Spring

Rain beats down,
roots stretch up.

They'll meet
in a flower.

— RAYMOND SOUSTER

The Red Wheelbarrow

so much depends
upon

a red wheel
barrow

glazed with rain
water

beside the white
chickens.

— WILLIAM CARLOS WILLIAMS

The Island

Wrinkled stone
like an elephant's skin
on which young birches are treading.

— LILLIAN MORRISON

In Passing

Open-backed dumpy junktruck
stacked full of old floor-fans,
unplugged, unsteady, undone,
free-whirling like kids' pinwheels
in a last fresh breeze —
What a way to go!

— Gerald Jonas

Water Lily

My petals enfold stamens of gold.
I float, serene, while down below

these roots of mine are deeply stuck
in the coolest most delicious muck.

— RALPH FLETCHER

Open-billed
gulls
fighting
for fish heads
creak
like
rusted
gates.

—X. J. Kennedy

Window

Night from a railroad car window
Is a great, dark, soft thing
Broken across with slashes of light.

— CARL SANDBURG

Little Orange Cat

Little orange cat,
you prowl
like a small tiger
(stalking what?)
in the field
of white daisies
and shining
buttercups.

— CHARLOTTE ZOLOTOW

Subway Rush Hour

Mingled
breath and smell
so close
mingled
black and white
so near
no room for fear.

— LANGSTON HUGHES

A *Happy Meeting*

Rain meets dust:
soft, cinnamon kisses.

Quick, noisy courtship,
then marriage: mud.

— JOYCE SIDMAN

Firefly July

When I was ten, one summer night,
The baby stars that leapt
Among the trees like dimes of light,
I cupped, and capped, and kept.

—J. Patrick Lewis

Sandpipers

Sandpipers run with
their needle beaks digging — they're
hemming the ocean.

— April Halprin Wayland

Bronze Age

In a dusty drawer I found the keys
to a farmhouse long torn down,
and rubbing fresh the metal of the bits
smelled the child's own fear and first pennies.

— ROBERT MORGAN

In the Field Forever

Sun's a roaring dandelion, hour by hour.
Sometimes the moon's a scythe, sometimes a silver flower.
But the stars! all night long the stars are clover.
Over, and over, and over!

— ROBERT WALLACE

Sea Trade

All night long
 the moonlit sea
  tosses white chrysanthemums
   to the rocky shore.

    All night long
   the rocky shore
  offers in return . . .
 tattered petals.

— PATRICIA HUBBELL

The Moon was but a Chin of Gold
A Night or two ago —
And now she turns Her perfect Face
Upon the World below —

— EMILY DICKINSON

What is it the wind has lost
that she keeps looking for
under each leaf?

—JIM HARRISON AND TED KOOSER

Screen Door

When fog blurs the morning,
Porches glisten, shingles drip.
Droplets gather on the green screen door.
"Look," they say to one another,
"Look how dry it is inside."

—JAMES STEVENSON

headline

A leaf on
the doorstep –
dont even

have to pick
it up to
know the news.

—CID CORMAN

In the alley, a
stray cat drinks the round white moon
from a rain puddle.

— Alice Schertle

Tall City

Here houses rise so straight and tall
That I am not surprised at all
To see them simply walk away
Into the clouds — this misty day.

— Susan Nichols Pulsifer

The first September breeze fluttered
across the tops
of the withered grass
and fall came tumbling in as
if someone had thrown
open a door.

— LIZ ROSENBERG

November Night

Listen . . .
With faint dry sound,
Like steps of passing ghosts,
The leaves, frost-crisp'd, break from the trees
And fall.

— Adelaide Crapsey

Between Walls

the back wings
of the

hospital where
nothing

will grow lie
cinders

in which shine
the broken

pieces of a green
bottle

— William Carlos Williams

Moonlight

Is
that
a
silver
spoon
hanging
below the
clouds or
just

moonlight?

—BRUCE BALAN

Old truck
you've picked up: kids,
hay for winter-bound cows,
brand-new furniture for neighbors,
now rust.

— Cynthia Pederson

34

Fog

The fog comes
on little cat feet.

It sits looking
over harbor and city
on silent haunches
and then moves on.

— CARL SANDBURG

Uses for Fog

to conquer skyscrapers
to make a magic cloak
to become thistledown

— EVE MERRIAM

37

Dust of Snow

The way a crow
Shook down on me
The dust of snow
From a hemlock tree

Has given my heart
A change of mood
And saved some part
Of a day I had rued.

— ROBERT FROST

Snow Fence

The red fence
takes the cold trail
north; no meat
on its ribs,
but neither has it
much to carry.

— TED KOOSER

The house-wreckers have left the door and a staircase,
now leading to the empty room of night.

— CHARLES REZNIKOFF

A wild winter wind
Is tearing itself to shreds
  On barbed-wire fences.

— RICHARD WRIGHT

Winter Twilight

On a clear winter's evening
The crescent moon

And the round squirrels' nest
In the bare oak

Are equal planets.

— ANNE PORTER

Night

The dark steep roofs chisel
The infinity of sky:

But the white moonlight gables
Resemble
Still hands at prayer.

— HERBERT READ

A welcome mat of moonlight on the floor. Wipe your feet before getting into bed.

—Jim Harrison and Ted Kooser

Acknowledgments

"Daybreak reminds us" and "headline" by Cid Corman from *Nothing/Doing*, copyright © 1999 by Cid Corman. Reprinted by permission of New Directions Publishing Corp.

"Spring" by Raymond Souster is reprinted from *Collected Poems of Raymond Souster* by permission of Oberon Press.

"The Red Wheelbarrow" and "Between Walls" by William Carlos Williams from *The Collected Poems: Volume I, 1909-1939*, copyright 1938 by New Directions Publishing Corp. Reprinted by permission of New Directions Publishing Corp.

"The Island" by Lillian Morrison. Excerpted from "Two Pictures" in *Whistling the Morning In* by Lillian Morrison. Copyright © 1992 by Lillian Morrison. Used by permission of Marian Reiner for the author.

"In Passing" by Gerald Jonas. Used by permission of the author.

"Water Lily" by Ralph Fletcher. Used by permission of the author.

"Open-billed" by X. J. Kennedy. Copyright © 1991 by X. J. Kennedy. First appeared in *The Kite That Braved Old Orchard Beach*, published by Margaret K. McElderry Books. Reprinted by permission of Curtis Brown Ltd.

"Window" and "Fog" from *Chicago Poems* by Carl Sandburg, copyright 1916 by Holt, Rinehart and Winston and renewed 1944 by Carl Sandburg, reproduced by permission of Houghton Mifflin Harcourt Publishing Company.

"Little Orange Cat" from *Everything Glistens and Everything Sings: New and Selected Poems*, copyright © 1987 by Charlotte Zolotow, reproduced by permission of Houghton Mifflin Harcourt Publishing Company.

"Subway Rush Hour" from *The Collected Poems of Langston Hughes* by Langston Hughes, edited by Arnold Rampersad with David Roessel, Associate Editor, copyright © 1994 by the Estate of Langston Hughes. Used by permission of Alfred A. Knopf, an imprint of the Knopf Doubleday Publishing Group, a division of Random House, Inc.

"A Happy Meeting" by Joyce Sidman. Copyright © 2014 by Joyce Sidman. Used by permission of the author.

"Firefly July" by J. Patrick Lewis. Used by permission of the author.

"Sandpipers" by April Halprin Wayland. Copyright © 2014 by April Halprin Wayland. Used by permission of the author.

"Bronze Age" by Robert Morgan. Used by permission of the author.

"In the Field Forever" by Robert Wallace from *Ungainly Things*. Copyright © 1968 by Robert Wallace. Used by permission of Christine Wallace.

"Sea Trade" by Patricia Hubbell. Copyright © 2014 by Patricia Hubbell. Used by permission of Marian Reiner for the author.

For Chuck Primozich —
everyone has a story; thanks for sharing yours.
P. B. J.

For Sybille
M. S.

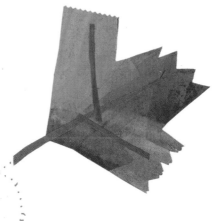

Compilation copyright © 2014 by Paul B. Janeczko
Illustrations copyright © 2014 by Melissa Sweet
Copyright acknowledgments appear on pages 46–47.

First edition 2014

Library of Congress Catalog Card Number 2013943087
ISBN 978-0-7636-4842-8

13 14 15 16 17 18 TLF 10 9 8 7 6 5 4 3 2 1

Printed in Dongguan, Guangdong, China

This book was typeset in Hightower.
The illustrations were done in watercolor, gouache, and mixed media.

Candlewick Press
99 Dover Street
Somerville, Massachusetts 02144

visit us at www.candlewick.com